D1409046

Walt Disney

Walt Disney

Academic Industries, Inc.
West Haven, Connecticut 06516

ISBN 0-88301-775-X

Published by
Academic Industries, Inc.
The Academic Building
Saw Mill Road
West Haven, Connecticut 06516

Printed in the United States of America

Walt Disney

Contents

Walt Disney's name is known all over the world. He gave life to Mickey Mouse and Donald Duck in some of the best cartoons of our time.

Watching his weekly television show was something millions of American families did together. This is the story of how Walt Disney came into their homes.

Born in Chicago in 1901, Walt was the fourth of five children. His father, Elias Disney, worked as a building contractor.

His mother, Flora, had been a teacher before she was married.

Newspaper
Boy
and Artist

When Walt was four years old, his family moved to a farm near Marceline, Missouri.

There was plenty of hard work to do on the farm. Elias made his children do their share.

The two oldest boys didn't like the work. So they left and went back to Chicago. But Walt loved the farm! He even had a pet pig!

C'mon, "Skinny!"

Walt's best friend was his brother Roy. Roy was eight years older than Walt.

Look, Roy! I made a picture of "Skinny!"

That's great!

Walt's father tried to make a living selling apples. After five years he knew he couldn't do it. So he sold the farm, and the family moved to Kansas City.

In Kansas City, Elias Disney bought a newspaper route of two thousand people. Roy and Walt worked for their father.

They got up at 3:30 AM and delivered the morning paper.

Come on, wake up!

During the winter, the snow was often up to Walt's nose.

B-r-r-r. It's cold!

I'll just rest a minute and get warm.

When Walt woke up, he delivered the rest of his papers and ran all the way to school.

He longed for the day when he wouldn't have to work for his father anymore.

A year passed. Roy finished high school and left home as his older brothers had done.

I wish I could go with you, Roy.

So do I, but you have to finish school.

So Walt stayed in school. He also delivered papers. But on Saturdays he went to art classes.

Very good, Walt.

Sometimes Elias Disney let his son go to the movies with a friend whose father owned a theater.

Why don't you wait

They saw "silent movies." The actors moved their lips to speak, and the audience read what they were saying at the bottom of the screen.

Then Walt worked out an act for the shows put on by people in his neighborhood. He used jokes he saw in the movies.

The
First Few
Art Jobs

In 1917, when the United States entered World War I, Elias Disney sold his paper route. Then he bought a jelly factory in Chicago. When the family moved, Walt stayed behind to finish school.

That summer he sold newspapers on the Santa Fe Railroad.

Get your papers here!

In the fall, he went to school in Chicago. He worked in the jelly factory and took art classes at night.

One day Walt got a letter from Roy. He was passing through Chicago on his way to a navy training camp. Roy asked Walt to meet him at the train station.

Gee, you've really grown!

They talked until Roy and the other recruits had to get on the train.

All aboard!

Talking to Roy gave Walt an idea.

19

Walt knew he had to be eighteen to join the navy. But he found out that the Red Cross Ambulance Corps took people who were seventeen.

Walt needed one of his parents to sign the papers. His father wouldn't sign, but his mother finally agreed.

Your name and age?

Walter Elias Disney, sir. Age seventeen.

Almost.

I'd rather know where you are than have you run off like the other boys.

The war ended while Walt was still training in Connecticut. But he was sent to France for a year to deliver supplies to the people there.

Walt returned to the United States in 1919. He went to Kansas City to look for work as an artist.

His first job was at Gray's Advertising Company. While working there, he met another young artist, Ub Iwerks.

By December, both Walt and Ub had lost their jobs.

Why don't we start our own business?

Sure! Why not?

A newspaper gave them an office. To pay the rent, Walt and Ub did artwork for the paper.

We got two orders today!

Then they heard of a job opening in a Kansas City film company.

Forty dollars a week! That's more than we both make together.

Why don't you take the job, Walt?

Later, the company also hired Ub.

In his job. Walt learned to make animated cartoons. He used cutout figures with parts that could be moved.

In his spare time, he used a borrowed camera to make his own cartoons.

He called them "Laugh-o-Grams." He was able to sell his cartoons to a nearby theater.

Soon Walt had enough money to start his own company.

For a while the office was a busy place.

Walt saved money by eating only once a day. At night he slept in his office.

But within a year the company failed. Young Walt Disney was broke.

Walt Disney
and
the Movie
Business

Finally, Walt bought a ticket to California. He wanted to get into the movie business. Also, he hoped to see his brother Roy who was in a hospital there.

When he left Kansas City, he had only forty dollars. He also had a short film called "Alice in Cartoonland" which he had made.

In Los Angeles, he rented a room from his uncle, Robert Disney. Then he began to look for a job with a motion picture company.

When he couldn't find a job, he rented an old camera and built a studio in his uncle's garage.

Finally, he found someone who wanted to buy "Alice in Cartoonland." He told Roy about it.

A man in New York wants twelve "Alice" films! He'll pay $1,500 for each one. Will you be my partner, Roy?

As soon as Roy was well, he and Walt borrowed five hundred dollars. They rented a tiny office, and started to work on the "Alice" films.

They took pictures of a little girl standing in front of a backdrop. Then Walt drew cartoons which were photographed   and printed on the film.

Roy had trouble cranking the old-fashioned camera at the same speed all the time.

The pictures jerk too much. We could sure use Ub Iwerks to run the camera.

So Walt wrote to Ub Iwerks in Kansas City and asked him to come out and help. Ub came in a hurry!

Look who's here!

Together they made more Alice cartoons. Soon more people came to work for them. Most of the money they made went into making better pictures.

We're lucky we don't eat much!

To save money, Walt and Roy rented an apartment together.

One new worker was a young woman named Lillian Bounds. Walt started driving her home after work.

Are you sure you won't come in for a minute?

Walt thought his clothes were too old. He didn't want to go in and meet Lillian's family.

Then one day . . .

Roy, we need new suits!

You're right! Edna and I are going to be married soon.

When Walt had his new suit, he went to Lillian's home and met her family.

Soon after Roy and Edna were married, there was another wedding.

Well, Lilly, what do you think we should pay for first—the car or the ring?

Walt and Lilly were married in July, 1925.

The company moved to a larger studio, and Walt and Lillian bought a house nearby.

After three years, Walt started work on a new character.

Here he is, boys— we'll use "Oswald the Rabbit" for our new animated cartoons!

The cartoon was very popular. Walt and Roy sold it to a man in New York.

We get $2,250 for each cartoon, but we can't make any money on that!

So Walt made a trip to New York to try to get more money for "Oswald the Rabbit."

I'm sorry, Mr. Disney, but we have to lower the price to $1,800 for your Oswald cartoons.

But I'll lose money!

I own Oswald the Rabbit, and I will make the cartoons myself. I'll even use some of your own artists.

Walt was sad that his artists would work for someone else.

From now on, Lilly, I'll make sure I own my characters.

Before boarding the return train for Los Angeles, Walt sent a message to Roy.

TELEGRAM

ROY: EVERYTHING O.K. COMING HOME. WALT

But that's not true!

I'll make it true.

On the train, Walt began working on a new character.

He's cute, but the name's not right!

MORTIMER MOUSE

So the mouse's name was changed to "Mickey."

When Walt got back to the studio, they began work on the new Mickey Mouse cartoons.

Soon afterward, Warner Brothers made an important movie called The Jazz Singer. It was the first successful "talking" picture.

Soon Walt and his people wrote the music for a Mickey Mouse cartoon called Steamboat Willy.

Walt showed the cartoon, and the artists added the music and sounds as they watched.

After a long search, they found a company to make the sound track for the cartoon. Walt himself did Mickey's voice.

Steamboat Willy was a hit. Soon there were four Mickey Mouse cartoons. They were shown in theaters all over the country.

Because Mickey Mouse was so popular, Walt's distributor wanted more money. But Walt knew this was not fair. So the distributor hired one of Walt's best men, Ub Iwerks, to draw cartoons for him.

We'll get another artist to do the mouse.

We've had problems before. Let's not worry about this one.

A few years later, Ub came back to work for the Disney studio.

But Walt was tired, and he worried about rising costs. He was often angry with his artists.

Do it over!

Finally, he went to a doctor. The doctor told him to take a vacation.

When he returned to work, he was his old self again.

During the 1930s, the Disney studio grew even larger. More people were hired, and Mickey Mouse's "gang" grew, too.

Pluto arrived in 1931, and Goofy followed a little later.

One day, Walt heard a man named Clarence Nash reading "Mary Had a Little Lamb" on the radio. He was using a voice that sounded like a duck.

Walt got Mr. Nash to come to the studio so the artists could hear him.

From that voice, they created Donald Duck. Donald first appeared in 1934.

Who me?

CHIP and DALE

Later, three young ducks and two chipmunks named Chip and Dale were added.

While Disney was making Mickey Mouse cartoons, he was also making films called "Silly Symphonies."

The first one was about some skeletons who rose from their graves and danced until dawn.

During this time Disney won two Academy Awards. One was for a Silly Symphony. The other was for his Mickey Mouse cartoons.

Walt's best-known Silly Symphony was The Three Little Pigs.

It was made at a time when many people were out of work.

18 MILLION JOBLESS: ROOSEVELT URGES AMERICANS TO STICK TOGETHER

"Who's afraid of the big bad wolf, the big bad wolf, the big bad wolf?"

THE THREE LITTLE PIGS
WALT DISNEY

The cartoon's happy message made people feel better. Some people even sang as they left the theater.

All Disney's films took hard work. A seven-minute cartoon required about 10,000 drawings.

The story was drawn by the artists, but they had writers, musicians and other people to help them.

One artist pinned sketches on the wall beside his desk. This way he could see the whole story at once.

Later, Walt started putting all the stories up this way. He called it the "story-board."

That looks like a good idea!

And this is where Mickey. . . .

Meanwhile, Mickey Mouse became even more popular.

There were Mickey Mouse ties, books, and watches with his picture on them. The whole world seemed to love Mickey Mouse.

In 1935, Walt Disney was honored for his work. He told newspaper reporters that he would soon make a much longer film.

The film will be *Snow White and the Seven Dwarfs.*

Snow White *took five years to make. It cost $1,750,000. Soon* Disney had 750 people working for him.

Some of his people even made a new kind of camera which made the cartoons better than earlier ones.

Not everyone thought Disney's film would be successful. But Walt had faith in it. Snow White and the Seven Dwarfs *earned eight and a half million dollars on its first run. Later, Walt decided to build a new studio.*

By the time it was finished in 1940, 1,500 people worked there.

Everyone liked the new studio, but the company now had other problems.

Some people get paid more than others for the same work.

On May 29, 1941, some people decided to strike against the Disney studio.

During the strike, the U.S. government sent Walt to South America to spread good will.

The strike was settled before he returned.

After the strike, Walt wasn't as close to the people who worked for him. But he was closer than ever to his family. He had two daughters, Diane and Sharon, whom he loved very much.

When Diane started school, she was surprised to learn that her father was a well-known man.

Daddy, are you the Walt Disney?

Why, yes, I guess I am.

One day, Walt took his daughters to an amusement park.

Why can't an amusement park be clean?

He began to dream of building a different kind of amusement park.

The
Amusement
Parks

But then the United States entered World War II. Disney had to cut back on all his work. The army even used part of his studio as one of its bases.

The army stayed for seven months. Then, for the next three years, the studio made films for the government. Not until after the war did work begin again on the new cartoons Cinderella, Alice in Wonderland, and Peter Pan.

On a trip to Alaska, Walt met two photographers named Edna and Al Milotte.

How would you like to do some movies about Alaska for me?

Walt liked their films about the lives of fur seals. He sent them a message.

TELEGRAM
EDNA AND AL:
MAKE MOVIES
OF FUR SEALS.
WALT

The Milottes lived for a year in the Pribiloff Islands doing just that.

They made a prize-winning movie called Seal Island.

Shortly after the movie about the seals, Disney made his first film using real people.

Treasure Island *was made in England.*

Finally, in 1952, Walt began to plan the amusement park of his dreams—Disneyland!

It's the craziest idea I ever heard!

In order to raise money for Disneyland, Walt agreed to do a weekly television show called Disneyland.

Born on a mountain-top in Tennessee . . .

Davy Crockett *was one of the popular stories shown on Dis-neyland.*

Walt also made a show called The Mickey Mouse Club.

M·I·C·K·E·Y M·O·U·S·E

Besides the Mousketeers, the show had stories like "Spin and Marty" and, of course, the Disney cartoons.

Disneyland finally opened in 1955. The park was built with the same care that went into the studio's work. It was a beautiful place.

Mr. Disney, you must be a very rich man.

Yes, I guess I am; they tell me I owe about ten million dollars!

Walt made sure that the park was kept clean and that the people who worked there were cheerful and polite to visitors.

Between 1950 and 1965, the Disney studio made sixty-two feature films. The most popular was Mary Poppins.

The movie won five Academy Awards. Walt Disney now had twenty-nine Academy Awards for his cartoon and movie work.

POCKET BIOGRAPHIES

Disney's last dream was Disney-world, a park like Disneyland to be built in Florida.

In 1966, Walt spent some time in a hospital. He talked to his visitors about plans for Disney-world.

It will be even better than Disneyland!

This is where we'll put the monorail.

Walt died on December 15, 1966, at the age of 65.

But Walt Disney's company goes on without him. As for his characters—Mickey, Donald and the rest—they may be sure of a long and happy future   in the hearts of people everywhere.

The END

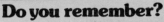

Do you remember?

As a child, Walt Disney worked hard for his father, who had:

a. a factory.   b. a newspaper route.   c. a store.

In his early films Walt used real people mixed in with cartoons. The first of these films was called:

a. *Alice in Cartoonland.*   b. *The Three Little Pigs.*
c. *Pinocchio.*

POCKET BIOGRAPHIES

Disney's first very popular character was:

a. Mickey Mouse.   b. Pluto.   c. Minnie Mouse.

Disney's first feature-length cartoon was:

a. *Donald Duck.*   b. *Little Lulu.*
        c. *Snow White and the Seven Dwarfs.*

Quiz
Yourself

(Answers at end of section)

Words to know

route   a series of places where a
person sells or delivers
something

actors   people who take part in
a movie or play

advertising the use of words and pictures
to sell a product

sound track the music for a movie or
cartoon put on a record
or tape

sketches   small, rough drawings

Can you use them?

Using the words above, complete the following sentences.

1. A movie's _____ must be good because what the
audience hears is as important as what it sees.

2. The movie was never finished
because the _____
wanted too much money.

3. After the artist showed his
_____ , he was
given the job right away.

4. Many young people earn
spending money by having a
paper _____ .

5. When _____ one
of its products, a company
must tell the truth.

49

Using pictures

In reading illustrated stories, you will find it helpful to "read" the pictures as well as the words. In this picture, you see young Walt Disney helping his older brother Roy on their Missouri farm. Walt always looked up to Roy. Now turn to pages 38, 39, 43, and 44. Find other pictures to show how Walt and Roy got along together.

While you are reading

As a boy and as a young man, Walt Disney had a hard life. He had many jobs—first to help his family, and later to earn money for himself. But he knew that one day his work would be rewarded. While you are reading, list the jobs Walt had before he became famous for his cartoons.

_____

_____

_____

_____

_____

_____

How well did you read?

When you have finished reading, answer the following questions.

1. What did Walt Disney call his first animated cartoons?

   (Check the correct answer.)

   _____ a.   "Mousecartoons"

   _____ b.   "Alice in Cartoonland"

   _____ c.   "Silly Symphonies"

   _____ d.   "Laugh-o-Grams"

2. Who was Walt Disney's first animal character?

   (Check the correct answer.)

   _____ a.   Mickey Mouse

   _____ b.   Pluto

   _____ c.   Oswald the Rabbit

   _____ d.   Donald Duck

POCKET BIOGRAPHIES

3. Who was responsible for naming Mickey Mouse?

(Check the correct answer.)

_____ a.   Lillian Disney

_____ b.   Roy Disney

_____ c.   Ub Iwerks

_____ d.   Walt Disney

4. After 1941, why wasn't Walt close to the people who worked for him?

(Check the correct _answers._)

_____ a.   Walt decided to turn the work of the studio over to his daughters.

_____ b.   The workers held a strike against the Disney studio.

_____ c.   Walt was so busy with other projects that he couldn't spend much time with his workers.

_____ d.   There were so many workers that Walt couldn't know them all.

_____ e.   Many of Disney's workers left to fight in World War II.

5. Which of the following are Disney movies?

   (Check the correct *answers.*)

____ a. *Treasure Island*

____ b. *Disney World*

____ c. *Seal Island*

____ d. *The Mouseketeers*

____ e. *Mary Poppins*

____ f. *The Jazz Singer*

Using what you've read

Choose your favorite Walt Disney movie. Write a summary of the story and explain why the movie is your favorite. Also, tell how the movie is like other Walt Disney movies you have seen. If it is different in any way, describe the differences, too.

WALT DISNEY

Can you use them?

1. sound track
2. actors
     5. advertising

3. sketches
4. route

How well did you read?

1. d
2. c
     5. a, c, e

3. a
4. b, c, d

NOTES

NOTES

NOTES

NOTES

COMPLETE LIST OF POCKET CLASSICS AVAILABLE

COMPLETE LIST OF POCKET CLASSICS AVAILABLE
(cont'd)

COMPLETE LIST OF POCKET CLASSICS AVAILABLE
(cont'd)

SHAKESPEARE

S 1 As You Like It
S 2 Hamlet
S 3 Julius Caesar
S 4 King Lear
S 5 Macbeth
S 6 The Merchant of Venice
S 7 A Midsummer Night's Dream
S 8 Othello
S 9 Romeo and Juliet
S10 The Taming of the Shrew
S11 The Tempest
S12 Twelfth Night

BIOGRAPHIES

B 1 Charles Lindbergh
B 2 Amelia Earhart
B 3 Houdini
B 4 Walt Disney
B 5 Davy Crockett
B 6 Daniel Boone
B 7 Elvis Presley
B 8 The Beatles
B 9 Benjamin Franklin
B10 Martin Luther King, Jr.
B11 Abraham Lincoln
B12 Franklin D. Roosevelt
B13 George Washington
B14 Thomas Jefferson
B15 Madame Curie
B16 Albert Einstein
B17 Thomas Edison
B18 Alexander Graham Bell
B19 Vince Lombardi
B20 Pelé
B21 Babe Ruth
B22 Jackie Robinson
B23 Jim Thorpe
B24 Althea Gibson